star stories

Sit down, get comfortable and read on, as we review some of the funniest reviews found online!

100% real, these funny, cheeky and just plain rude stories will have you in hysterics, clicking 'add to basket' through the tears!

books by
BOXER

www.booksbyboxer.com

Published in the UK by
Books By Boxer, Leeds, LS13 4BS
© 2020 Books By Boxer
All Rights Reserved
Printed In China

ISBN: 9781909732711

star
stories

BS Banana Slicer
Saved my marriage
By <u>Mrs K</u>

What can I say about the BS Banana Slicer that hasn't already been said about the wheel, penicillin, or the iPhone... this is one of the greatest inventions of all time.

My husband and I would argue constantly over who had to cut the day's banana slices. It's one of those chores NO ONE wants to do! You know, the old "I spent the entire day rearing OUR children, maybe YOU can pitch in a little and cut these bananas?" and of course, "You think I have the energy to slave over your damn bananas? I worked a 12 hour shift just to come home to THIS?!" These are the things that can destroy an entire relationship.

It got to the point where our children could sense the tension. The minute I heard our 6-year-old girl in her bedroom, re-enacting our daily banana fight with her dolls, I knew we had to make a change. That's when I found the BS Banana Slicer. Our marriage has never been healthier, AND we've even incorporated it into our lovemaking. THANKS BS BANANA SLICER!

> Cheaper than a marriage councillor, this banana slicer seems to have worked wonders on this reviewer's marriage... Though I can't even begin to imagine how you'd use a banana slicer in your love making!
> 4 stars for your strong relationship with your husband (and banana slicer?!)

<u>Amazon</u> USA

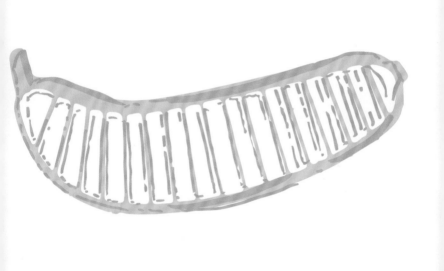

Noise Cancelling Headphones
Noise ELIMINATING!
By  Anon

★ ★ ★ ★ ★

So, not so funny story....

Someone in the apartment unit above us got STABBED. According to the cop who interviewed us, the attacker rang the upstairs doorbell, and when the guy answered the attacker forced his way in and stabbed the guy. You want to know what the scary part is? I didn't hear a thing, thanks to my amazing Noise Cancelling Headphones. I got them on Amazon for only $99.99! (free shipping). These things work as advertised!

Probably the best noise cancelling headphones I've ever owned.

10/10 would buy again.

The one regret from this situation is that your neighbour was too late purchasing these noise cancelling headphones! Though at $99.99, it might be cheaper to just ignore the doorbell...
5 stars, hoping your neighbour makes a full recovery!

Cow Butter Dish
Udderly Worthless
By Dairy Queen

Looks good, nicely made but.... Is too small to house a block of butter! Why, oh, why didn't I read the other reviews before buying??????

I think I was seduced by the relaxed look of the cow and just assumed a butter dish would be a great place to store my un-eaten butter.

I now have a dull square one from Tesco that was only £4 and the cow of shame is hidden in a cupboard. I'm too embarrassed to give it away and too cheap to chuck it.

Thinking about it now it may make a nice passive aggressive present for someone you don't like.

> Dairy me! What a dilemma this is... Don't start beefing though, maybe cut down your block of butter just margarinely? Otherwise I'm sure you can use this amoosing butter dish for something else...
> 2 stars. Stop spreading disappointment!

Where Is Baby's Belly Button

DO NOT buy this book, you can SEE the ending right on the cover!

By <u>Justin</u>

This book is completely misleading. The entire plot revolves around finding Baby's belly button; the title makes this much clear from the beginning.

However there is no mystery. There is no twist. Baby's belly button is right where it's supposed to be, on Baby's stomach. Right where it clearly SHOWS you it is on the COVER OF THE BOOK.

This plot is a complete mess as a result of its reliance on the mystery of where the belly button is; everything falls apart the second you realize that the belly button was in plain sight all along. There is no conflict, there is no character development, and there is scarcely any plot.

Whoever wrote this book must have a serious error in judgement, because you would have to be an infant to not immediately understand where Baby's belly button is.

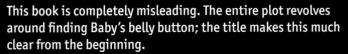

How dare that baby have his belly button on their BELLY! Oh the audacity! I guess in this case you really can judge a book by its cover... I'm so disappointed that I don't want to play peek-a-boo anymore. 1 star for ruining the story for me... I was getting to the good part too.

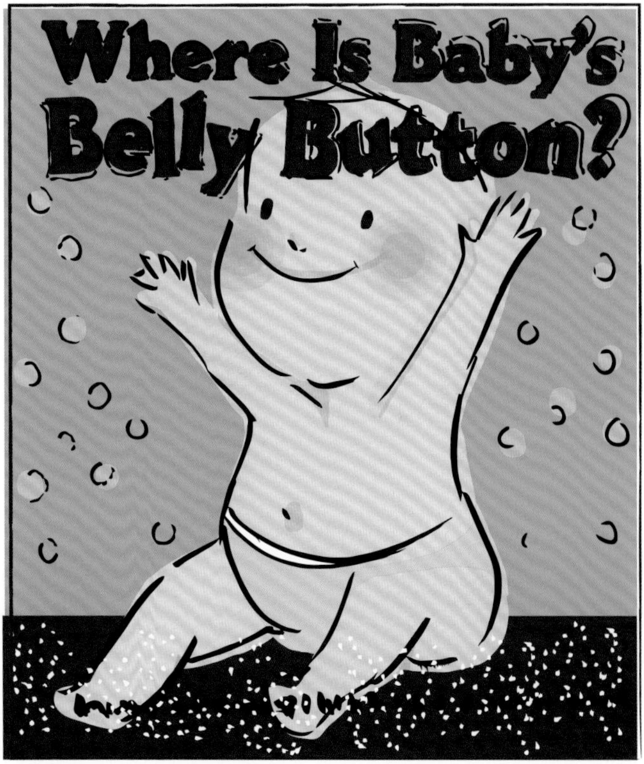
Where Is Baby's Belly Button?

Robot Vacuum
Very disappointed!
By T. M. Best

Very disappointing! We named ours Bob, and let me tell you he wasn't the hard working man I was hoping for. Bob spent most of his employment driving from one random side of the house to the other like a junkie looking for his next fix.

His actual cleaning was minimal at best and he couldn't find his docking station to save his life. In the week I had Bob he never finished a cleaning cycle. One day while at work the app texted me to say Bob needed my assistance because he was stuck on a cliff.

Worried for Bob's safety I came home to find him passed out in the middle of the dining room rug. That night the family said goodbye to Bob once and for all.

What did you expect from a robot with a man's name? Didn't you learn from the man of the house that they do minimal work and want all the rewards? Poor Bob only wants to sit and watch his football with a nice cold beer...
2 stars for not doing it yourself.

Amazon UK

Crafting With Cat Hair
Worked like a charm
By Rico

I purchased this book as I was tired of people sitting too near me on public transport.

No eye contact, no questions. Perfect.

While this review certainly will have the crazy old cat ladies hissing and spitting furballs, I for one love the idea of avoiding contact with overly friendly passengers on public transport.
3 stars!

Amazon UK

CRAFTING WITH CAT HAIR
Cute Handicrafts to Make with Your Cat

Yodelling Pickle
Better than Bieber
By Aunt Lynne

★ ★ ★ ★ ★

My twelve year-old niece asked for the Justin Bieber CD for Christmas, so I bought her this yodelling pickle.

Nobody can tell the difference so far.

Yodel-Ay-Ee-WHO?? Why would a twelve year old girl want a Justin Bieber CD when they can have their very own yodelling pickle?!
A 5 star aunt you are!

How to Avoid Huge Ships
WHY NO KINDLE EDITION?!?!?
By 1000 leagues

Given that there is a huge ship bearing down on me RIGHT NOW!

I am extremely disappointed that I cannot get inst......

Surely an audiobook is a much better edition. You can even hear the sound effects of the ship crashing through the waves, blowing its foghorn and even the captain screaming to move out of the way... Oh wait!
4 sta.......

 USA

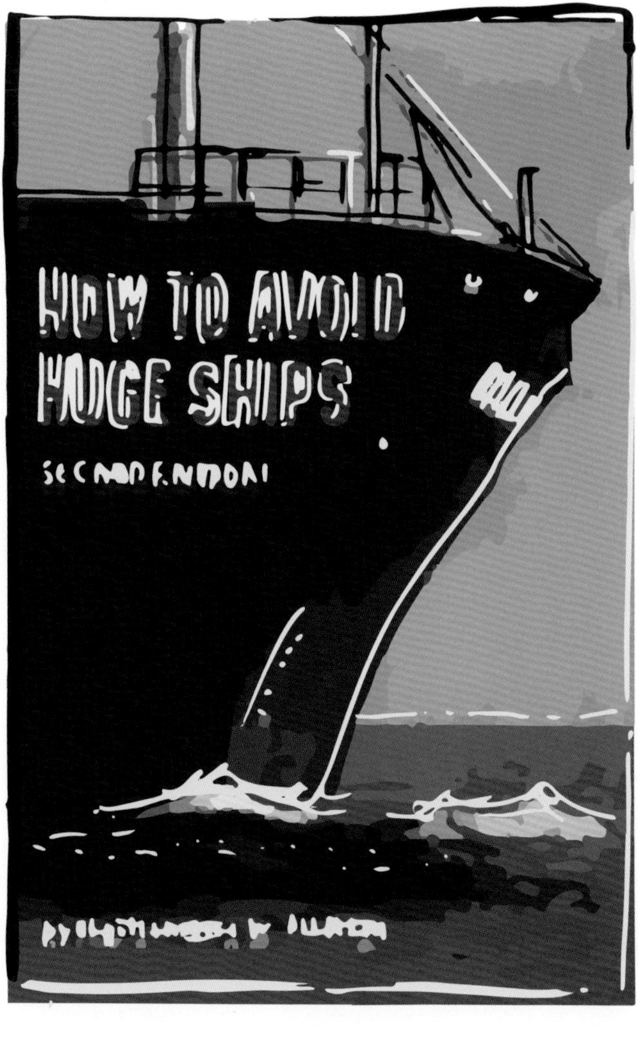
HOW TO AVOID HUGE SHIPS
SECOND EDITION

Car Dashboard Reflector
Really hard to drive with...
By Joshuwaaaah

I love this product. It keeps my car nice and cool, BUT I will say that the only defect I have found so far is that it is very hard to drive with this on. I have had over 5 wrecks since I purchased it.

After my first fender bender, I decided it was best to roll down the window and stick my head out to see the road, but even that is hard because my eyes and mouth dry out very quickly. Since then, I have purchased some swimming goggles and a snorkel which has helped out tremendously during long drive.

If you get stopped by the police, just show them this review and you're sure to be free to go with no charges AND get the police department raving about their brand new dashboard Reflectors! WIN, WIN! 5 stars – one for each of your wrecks.

Amazon USA

10ft Wide Beach Ball
Fun way to ruin a weekend.
By <u>Too tired to run</u>

We took this ball to the beach and after close to 2 hours to pump it up, we pushed it around for about 10 fun filled minutes. That was when the wind picked it up and sent it hurtling down the beach at 40 knots.

It destroyed everything in its path. Children screamed in terror at the giant inflatable monster that crushed their sand castles. Grown men were knocked down trying to save their families. The faster we chased it, the faster it rolled. It was like it was mocking us. Eventually, we had to stop running after it because its path of injury and destruction was going to cost us a fortune in legal fees.

Rumor has it that it can still be seen stalking innocent families on the Florida panhandle. We lost it in South Carolina, so its clearly durable.

Known as one of the worst disasters in history, the South Carolina catastrophe is a world-known event that will haunt us for years to come. Quite like King-Kong and Godzilla, the abominable beach ball destroys anything in its path and reigns terror on those around.
For its durability though, the review AND the beach ball gets 5 stars!

<u>Amazon</u> USA

NYX Professional Makeup
I was hit by a car
By Sorefia

I was hit by a car and through the hit itself, the rain, the ambulance ride, and the hours in the hospital my makeup stayed completely intact the entire time.

When I was discharged from the hospital I had to take off my makeup and none of it had moved. If this setting spray can survive being hit by a car then that's all the proof I need and I'll definitely be buying it again!

Why is this a review for makeup and not on car maintenance products? If it stays perfectly in place on your face, then perhaps it'll keep your car intact after a bump or two!
4 dizzy stars (maybe its concussion...)

Facebook USA

Long Lasting Dog Bone
Disappointment all round.
By  Terry

★ ★ ☆ ☆ ☆

Dear Company Owner,

Your "long lasting" bone lasted all of 5 minutes.

If that's your idea of a long lasting bone then I feel sorry for your wife!

For a bone that lasts 2 minutes and 30 seconds longer than most men, I can't see what this reviewer has against this doggie treat! Though they might feel the need to chew out the creators of this bone, I'm pretty sure their pooch will say otherwise!
Give the dog a bone (and 3 stars)

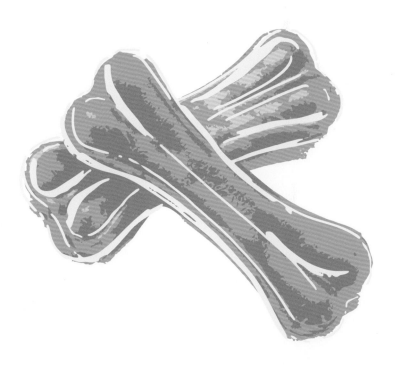

Santa Hat and Beard
Eyebrows for the eyebrow santa
By Grey Ham

The beard is sewn directly to the hem of the hat, which means that the eye-hole is (on the normal sized head) positioned directly over the forehead.

This is fantastic if you're aiming to dress as a Santa Claus with locked-in syndrome who can only communicate via the wiggling of his eyebrows, but most would probably describe that as more depressing than festive.

Though he might not see you while you're sleeping, I'm sure Santa Brows will be putting this reviewer on the naughty list for this cheeky explanation.
(And people wonder why children cry at the grotto....)
4 stars and a cookie for this review!

Canned Unicorn Meat
Suspicious texture
By  50% Alive

★ ★ ☆ ☆ ☆

Unfortunately, I found this unicorn meat brand to be quite similar to spam, both in texture and blandness. I'd been hoping for that zestier kick that comes from the rump cuts of other mythical and fantastical creatures, such as griffins or centaurs (for the latter, serve only the back half of the creature with guests, or it gets awkward). Apparently, as Dateline recently reported, 'farmed' unicorns are force fed mostly genetic modified grains, rather than their natural diet of skittles and ecstasy pills. California in fact is ready to ban the practice and sale of such meat by referendum.

Moreover, certain European countries were caught mixing regular horse meat (yes, disgusting) so you never really know how pure the unicorn is. I say stick with fresh. I highly recommend TOM RIDDLE brand unicorn steaks, which arrive still oozing restorative blood.

> Has nobody ever told you not to buy food online? You get all kinds of unwanted bits in them... I once found a crunchy fairy wing in my mermaid pie. Though I must try the Tom Riddle unicorn steak with a glass of volde-port sometime. 5 stars for this gourmet reviewer!

Sugar Free Gummy Bears
Flying through!
By Confused and afraid

Not long after eating about 20 of these all hell broke loose. I had a gastrointestinal experience like nothing I've ever imagined. Cramps, sweating, bloating beyond my worst nightmare. I've had food poisoning from some bad shellfish and that was almost like a skip in the park compared to what was going on inside me.

Then came the, uh, flatulence. Heavens to Murgatroyd, the sounds, like trumpets calling the demons back to Hell... the stench, like 1,000 rotten corpses vomited. I couldn't stand to stay in one room for fear of succumbing to my own odors. What came out of me felt like someone tried to funnel Niagara Falls through a coffee straw. I swear my sphincters were screaming. It felt like a flood of toxic waste. 100% liquid. Flammable liquid. NAPALM. I felt violated when it was all over, which I think might have been sometime in the early morning of the next day. There was stuff coming out of me that I ate at my wedding 5 years ago.

> What do you expect when you eat tiny, defenceless gummy bears? Watching you bite off their sugar-free bear friends' heads without a sign of remorse.
> The surviving gummies said 3 stars... and diarrhoea is the least of your worries...

Amazon USA

The Chambong
Riggity-wrecked
By Amazon Customer

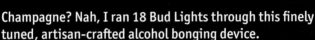

Champagne? Nah, I ran 18 Bud Lights through this finely tuned, artisan-crafted alcohol bonging device.

Whilst on my roof.

All in all, if you're trying to get riggity-wrecked with the most class possible, this is just for you!

What we really want to know is how on earth you perfected getting down from your roof in one piece after drinking 18 bud lights, with your arms still intact enough to be able to write a review?
3 stars for your concussion!

Amazon USA

LED Weighing Scale
This Scale - A poem
By lowendmadness

As I stepped on the glass
A blue light caught my eye
As the digital numbers
Began to climb so high
And just then it hit me
As I looked at my weight
That my body is fat
But this scale is great.

Reviewing a review
Is usually a farce
Especially when the product
Looks like something from mars
So for a rating on scales
That weigh your fat arse
My only option
Is to give it 5 stars.

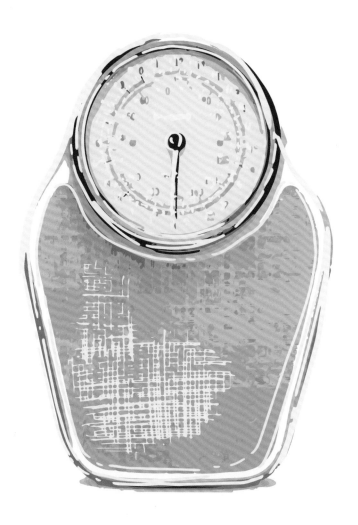

Interior Pet Door
Sneak Attack
By HWHL

★ ★ ★ ★ ☆

I hate my wife's cat but it made my wife pretty happy that the cat can come into our bedroom at-will now and claw the dogs while they sleep.

I hate that cat, but his door is pretty cool.

This review would be purrfect if only the reviewer liked cats. Cats are gentle creatures. Sweet, loving and full of ideas to take over the world. They even jump on your keyboard when you try to typ-hbfgn-jll-1star-jkdsnv.

Amazon UK

Senior Woman Inhaler Decal
Finally suitable decor!
By <u>Ashley Wan</u>

My husband and I have been arguing about what to fill the large wall on the stairs with for months. He wanted a mirror, I wanted a large image of an old woman using an inhaler. Having always been a little bit of a boundary pusher and decor daredevil, he's always come up with these odd suggestions. A mirror, ha!

When he suggested it, I actually laughed in his face. Then I told my friends who also laughed. One questioned why I married him. She actually gave me the idea in the first place as she has a large decal above her fireplace, a beautiful piece named 'man with hearing aid.' It's like you can almost see him tweak at the volume.

Real Art.

Breath-taking. A review that will make you gasp at its honesty. I'm blown away at the thought of the reviewer's husband wanting a measly mirror on the wall instead of art like this.
4 stars for this reviewers taste in décor.

<u>Amazon</u>USA

Ergonomic Wrist Rest
The development meeting...
By  B. O. Nun

⭐ ⭐ ⭐ ⭐ ⭐

""Thanks for joining me today team. We need to come up with the packaging design for our Ergonomic Wrist Rest."

"What is our target market?"

"Primarily people with weak/injured wrists. I would expect a large amount of them to have Arthritis."

"Ok. Shall we wrap it in plastic and cardboard and make it impossible to open?"

"Yes. Ideal. Use all the glue."

"How much glue?"

"Every last drop we have. Make those limp-wristed, weaklings suffer.""

> I'd love to type more of a review for this, however I injured my wrist in a totally unrelated packaging opening incident. Damn these CEO's, flaring up our arthritis one package at a time!
> 3 stars... one for every finger I've cracked!

Half Keyboard
A great bard!
By  A. Wf

⭐ ⭐ ⭐ ⭐ ⭐

Das bard es ver gad!

A've traed et far tree weex ad et werx great!

A recabed et ta aw Agazad watcxers!

Fave stars!!!!

50 HPPY YOU LIK IK.
I think we might have received the other side of your keyboard by mistake. While it certainly types, I don't think even the best codebreakers could manage to read through that without getting a slight headache.
3 stars for effort, though!

Classic Ouija Board Game
WARNING!
By Amazon Customer

Tried to summon Satan.

MOTHER IN LAW SHOWED UP!

Not worth the risk.

> Short and sweet but ghoulishly informative, this review tells us
> everything we need to know about the quality of this spooky board.
> Let's hope they said goodbye or she'll be haunting them forever!
> 3 Stars
> G.O.O.D.B.Y.E.

Mens Cargo Shorts
Too revealing.
By <u>Bill Baggs</u>

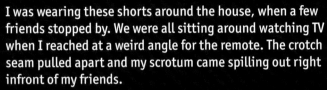

I was wearing these shorts around the house, when a few friends stopped by. We were all sitting around watching TV when I reached at a weird angle for the remote. The crotch seam pulled apart and my scrotum came spilling out right infront of my friends.

This was pretty embarrassing. Picture not attached.

When buying cheap cargo shorts online, you might also want to consider buying some cheap underpants as well! While this review contains a little too much information, it definitely describes the quality of the product... (And the horror of his friends, too)
I'll give bill and his balls 4 stars.

<u>Amazon</u> USA

AA Batteries
Would not buy again!
By Suffolk Cating

I put these batteries in my carbon monoxide detector and they do not work!

As soon as I put them in the alarm would not stop!

Have you tried turning it off and on again? I bet it's giving you a real banging headache! I wouldn't hold your breath for a refund though... This review is so short-winded that I can only give it 2 stars!

Amazon UK

Large Casket
Fit for purpose
By I. Afortyoone

No complaints from Grandpa.

Though people are dying to get into one, you'll be digging a hole if you buy this as a gift for somebody. Let's hope Grandpa didn't make a grave mistake!
5 stars for Grandpa's grave.
Review in Peace

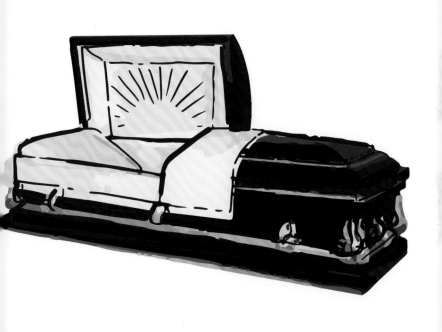

Book of Immortality
I died.
By 6 feet down

This book didn't work at all.

Wait.....

With your new found powers of immortality, I'd have expected more than a 7 word review for a book that can cheat death... If I give you 5 stars, can I 'borrow' it?

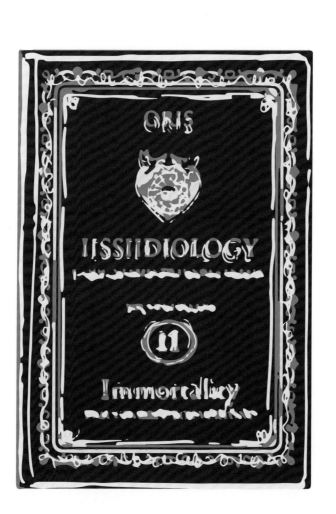

16999 Swiss Army Knife

So close to perfection.

By Amazon customer

⭐ ☆ ☆ ☆ ☆

I tried to file my nails, but in the process I accidentally fixed a small engine that was nearby. That was nice.

However I am dismayed to find out this product has no banana slicer - that's a deal breaker. Returning today.

Have you tried building a banana slicer with your 16999 Swiss Army Knife? When you find the right tool for the job, that is.
How can you give a bad review for a tool that does almost everything? 2 stars for your pickiness!

Amazon **USA**

Uranium Ore
Unfortunate side effects
By  Dr. Serp

★ ★ ★ ★ ☆

I left this product next to my pet lizard, unfortunately now he's 350 feet tall and is currently destroying Tokyo.

I got a free box labelled "cat" but I'm not sure I should open it to see if it is OK.

Will it be glow in the dark? Will it have two heads? Don't leave us in suspense!
Open the box and tell us what's inside, then we might give you 5 stars...

Dancing With Cats
My cat was never a dancer.
By Kristi

My cat was never a dancer. An artist? Maybe. A rapper? Of course! But a dancer, she would have none of that. I read this book to my cat every night for one year. She cried through most of it. She still won't dance with me.

Maybe it's not the quality of the book you should be reviewing but the quality of your mew-sic. Have you tried some kitty classics like 'What's New Pussycat?' or 'Cool for Cats'?
I'm feline like this review is worth 4 stars just because you tried.

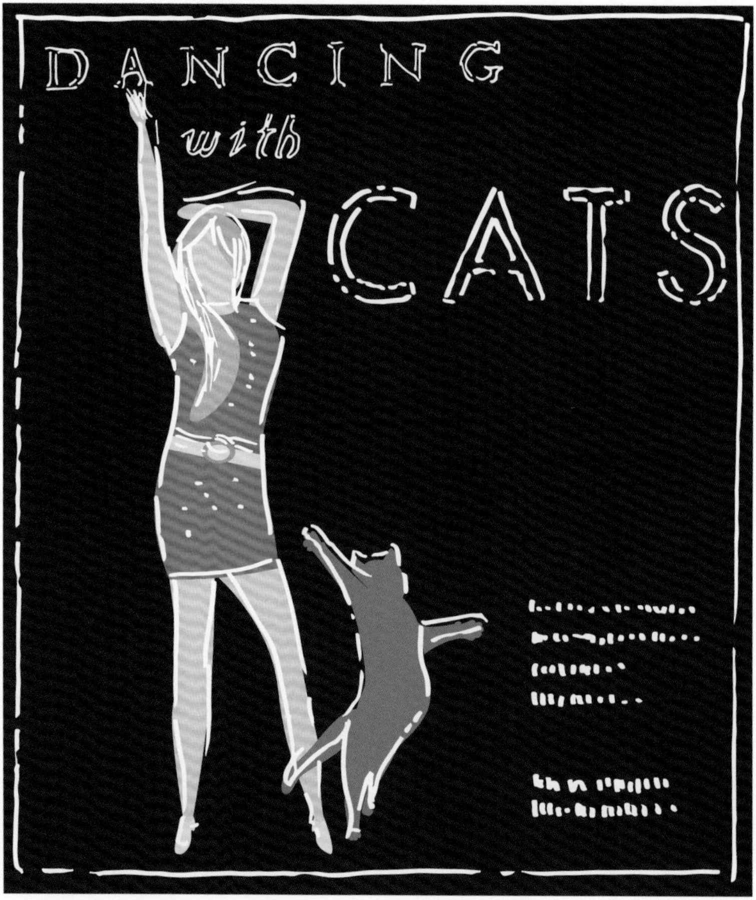
DANCING
with
CATS

Latex Rooster Mask
Great Quality!
By CluckingAround

⭐ ⭐ ⭐ ⭐ ⭐

When I received this my wife was at work. I waited until she was getting ready for work the next morning and put it on with my face right in front of hers while she was blow drying her hair with her eyes closed.

When she opened them and saw me she screamed like I've never heard her scream and punched me in the arm.

HARD. So yeah, it's a great quality mask.

We can all agree that this rooster mask is clucking amazing! This reviewer wasn't playing chicken when he scared his wife and put her in a fowl mood.
5 stars for bravery (and because the mask is egg-cellent), we hope your arm didn't ache too much.

Inflatable Beard
Inflataphrodisiac
By  Amazon Customer

⭐ ⭐ ⭐ ⭐ ⭐

You never know when you are going to find that one perfect accessory that women can't seem to take their eyes off of. Last year it was the fanny-pack designed to be worn UNDER your pants.

This year the inflatable beard is going to make last year seem like a bad dream. This 'inflataphrodisiac' (a word that everyone who buys one of these will understand the minute he stares persistently at a strange woman in an elevator) is the perfect accompaniment to my inflatable chest-hair wig. I feel like manliness coated in ruggedness and wrapped in bacon.

For convenience, it's easily removable at the beach, when scrubbing in for surgery, or when 'things get intimate' (but if she wants you to leave it on....and she might....it can be sprayed off with a garden hose afterwards). But please remember, THIS IS NOT A FLOATATION DEVICE.

> I've never seen anyone be so impressed with a real beard, never mind an inflatable one! I highly doubt this reviewer will be picking up any inflatable beard fangirls any time soon though...
> An inflated 3 stars for this inflataphrodisiac!

<u>100 Googly Eyes</u>
Brings the town to life
By <u>Rachel</u>

I'm 25. I bought these so that I could drunkely wander my college town at night, appending them in hilarious places (i.e those tacky lions in front of frat houses). My plan worked BRILLIANTLY with one tiny hiccup....

the backs of the smaller eyes are killer to get off, even with longer nails (and even sober - I tried that too). As a result I suffered minor injuries on my right thumbnail.

Totally worth it though!

There's more than what meets the eye with this review. While the reviewer gave a pretty accurate description of these googly eyes, eyebrows are raised at what other objects were given eyeballs against their will.
2 stars (one for each eye)

<u>Amazon</u> USA

Medium Rectangular Sponge
New friends!!!
By NoLongerAlone

If I could give these sponges a MILLION STARS! I would.

I love them so much, I couldn't even bring myself to use them, so I drew faces on them! They are now my friends!

I have a little over 40 sponges friends and I am soon ordering more. I LOVE THESE SPONGES!!

They are a gift from god!

While we're happy that this reviewer is making friends, we want to know how well the sponge washes, not talk to them about last night's soap opera! That being said, don't wet your little friends or their faces might smudge...
4 stars for cuteness overload!

Amazon USA

Penguin Mask
Sweet Lullabies
By Kinguin

★ ★ ★ ★ ☆

I wear this mask to sing lullabies to my children. They are terrified of the mask. Whenever they protest about their bedtime, or ask for too many sweets, I whip on the mask and they soon know who is the King Penguin.

1 star removed for fishy smell.

This reviewer sure knows how to make a fun mask terrifying! While their kids scream in tune to twinkle, twinkle, they should be adding that star back for fishy scent authenticity!
5 stars for putting this slightly creepy mask to good use.

Amazon USA

Horse Head Mask

Neigh sayers
By Amazon Customer

⭐ ⭐ ⭐ ⭐ ⭐

I purchased this mane-ly for anonymity, but instead it was a night-mare that saddled me with un-bridled panic. At a recent Comic Con, I donned the mask wearing my best track suit, jockeying for a simple laugh: 'What do gay horses eat?' I queried, eager to bray 'Heeeeeyyyy!!' Comic gold, friends, I know.

But neigh-sayers came unglued. 'No! You're George Takei! I know that voice!'

Now, it doesn't take a gallop poll to know what happened next. I hoofed it out of there with herds of fans riding my ass, shouting till they, too, were... horse.

This review took me on a wild ride from start to finish. Some may tell the reviewer to get off their high horse and stop foaling around, but I say there was stable humour and criticism throughout.
The real question? Yay or neigh......
I'd give this review a galloping 5 stars!

Set of Tiny Hands
Tiny love
By

⭐ ⭐ ⭐ ⭐ ⭐

There aren't enough words to express my gratitude for these tiny hands.

They have made me closer with my friends, they have brought me peace of mind, and, most importantly, they have strengthened my relationship with God.

After reading this review I had to purchase my very own pair of tiny hands. I'm now a member of the Miniature Church of Hands, praying daily to the gods so they can bless us with adorable tiny fingers! 5 stars... one for each finger and a thimble sized thumb!

Amazon USA

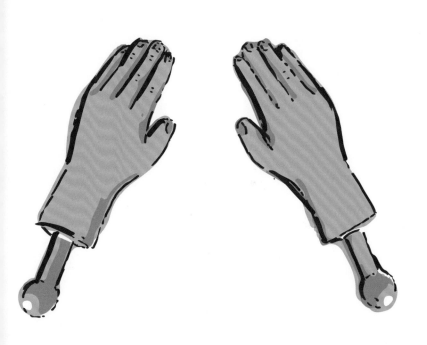

Steering Wheel Tray
A real experience!
By Amazon customer

★ ★ ★ ★ ★

My husband Brad always warns me not to try and update my Facebook page while I'm driving.

'You'll hit another pedestrian,' he says. 'This isn't the Enterprise, there isn't a deflector array.'

Then along comes a miracle product like this! I can now happily fly at warp speed down the streets of Los Angeles, laptop or mobile device perched right in front of me, so I can keep both eyes right on it AND on the road. It's so much easier to ignore all the frightened screams and annoying honking when you've got Facebook to look at while driving.

Thank you!

What's that I can hear? Screaming? Tires screeching? What does Brad know about good quality trays anyway? This reviewer has tried and tested this 'convenient' car accessory and just about survived to tell the tale!
0 stars for texting while driving though... tut tut

Amazon USA

Tolerance Vinyl Sticker
Good quality but...
By Amazon Customer

★ ★ ★ ★ ☆

I think it is a very nice piece, and seems to be made with good quality. However, most of the people do not now what it stands for, and I have been told it looks like a penis.

Don't tolerate the haters! I think this peni- *cough cough* pin sticker is very informative!
This review is certainly worth 3=Definite stars...

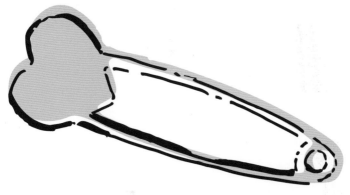

STANDING UP
TO INTOLERANCE

Rainbow Cloud Cookie Cutter
Was nice of her to say
By Failing to rise

★ ★ ★ ★ ★

Cutter is great but no matter what I did, I couldn't get the cookie dough to rise. My wife said "Oh, honey. It's ok. It happens to all bakers now and then."

Which, you know, was nice of her to say. Still, I felt kind of deflated.

I'm not sure why so many reviews are complaining about the size being too big. 5" x 3 $\frac{3}{4}$ " seems about average to me.

Finally! Someone who can appreciate a few inches of fun-filled baking! Little advice for the reviewer though, if you're still struggling to get it to rise to the occasion, you might need professional help.
Don't feel let down, we'll give you 3 stars for your passion!

Amazon USA

60 Condoms
Think ahead!
By

★ ★ ★ ★ ★

So these are some great condoms right, but I'm just here to give you some life advice.

I bought these back when I was in a relationship with someone way out of my league. I figured, after how long we have been together I should just start buying protection in bulk, right?

So I buy sixty condoms and we keep getting it on for a while until she dumped me. Now I have a drawer by my bed full of completely superfluous condoms. They sit there mocking me as I drunkenly cradle myself to sleep, cold and alone in my pathetic excuse of an apartment.

Great product though 10/10

Perhaps it was the outrageous drawer full of condoms that turned her off? Maybe it was the act itself? Whatever the case, this pitiful reviewer and his superfluous collection of rubbers gets a disappointing 3 stars!

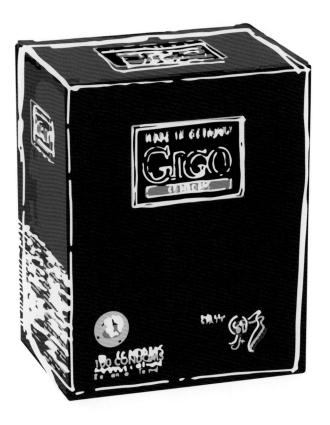

1L Flavourless Lube
Good lube
By <u>Slip n Slide</u>

It's lube, not much more to say...

Sometimes I like covering my body in it and pretend to be a slug while sliding around my bathroom.

This review has left me with more questions than answers. How much lube does it take for one to become a slug? Can slugs even write reviews? Mind-blowing!
A slithery slimy 5 stars!

<u>Amazon</u> UK

How to Poo on a Date
Misleading....
By Spike

I am somewhat disappointed.

Despite reading this book from cover to cover, my date still refuses to let me poo on her.

> It's not the book that's misleading but your date... How does she expect your relationship to go to the next level if you can't splash out on her? 5 stars... dump the girl and buy yourself a toilet seat instead.
> I pooped on a date once...

Amazon USA

Gentleman's Willy Care Kit
Stray hairs
By MrsMagarita

I bought this for my husband as I was so tired of trying to find the pork sword beneath all the reeds...

Low and behold, this kit actually worked and made his man parts so much more attractive.

It worked so well in fact, my husband became stripper, found a stripper girlfriend. I am now husband-less and blame the kit for everything!

Darn you Gentlemen's Willy Care Kit!!!! I want my unkempt willied husband back!

> Funny, I could have sworn I've seen a similar review about a man whose wife left him to become a stripper due to some cheap wax strips from amazon... Said he wanted his wife and her overgrown bush back...
> 4 stars for the broken heart...

UFO Detector
Still happening
By PhoneHome

This little gizmo is a bargain at twice the price and much more accurate than the voices in my head.

I am however still being abducted by UFO's on a regular basis.

May I suggest upgrading to a better quality tin foil hat to keep them pesky aliens at bay? It particularly works if you add pipe cleaner antennas too!
4 stars from the aliens on mars!

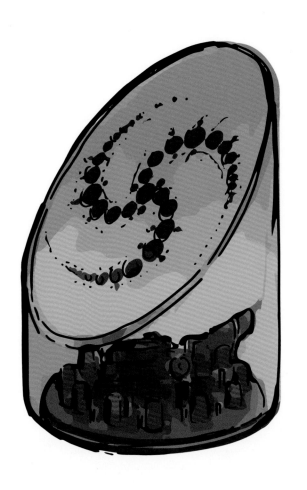

Knuckle Blaster Stun Gun
Sneak Attack
By <u>NotSteve</u>

I purchased this after I was confronted by some punks demanding that I hand over my money. I'm a relatively fit guy, but I was no match for them. That is when I realized that I need to protect myself. The day after I bought this product I went to the very same Wal-Mart parking lot when I was first mugged. I approached the group of hooligans standing outside the entrance, concealing my secret weapon.

I cooly asked "Remember me?".
One of them looked up and said, "Have you come back to buy some Samosas or Thin Mints? My Girl Scout Troops need to raise more money!"
I replied with "you're not taking my money this time". "But sir, they're delicious!", she said.

I whipped out my Knuckle Blaster Stun Gun hand and shouted "WRONG MOVE B****!" The five girl scouts ran away screaming.

> Damn those pesky girl scouts, pressuring us into buying cookies and supporting their menacing projects! This review shows us how such a little device can stop you being robbed of your hard earned cash!
> 5 stars and a cookie!

<u>Amazon</u> USA

A Million Digits
What a rip off!
By

⭐ ☆ ☆ ☆ ☆

I bought this book and waited, with baited breath, for the right moment. I figured (geddit?) an hour at home alone, with the lights turned down low, was all I needed to really take in the full glory of this mighty tome.

So imagine my disappointment when the time arrived, I cracked open the prize and found that there are NO SODDING 3's!!!

I know the million digits are random, but you'd have thought that somewhere in there a 3 would pop up. But no - not one of the little blighters.

Whoever proof-read this book should be on the sharp end of a stern talking-to. Quite frankly, it's not good enough, and now I feel ripped off.

> I just can't tally up how so many random variations can be missing the figure three. Then again, I don't think I'll ever add up why anyone would want to pay for a book full of digits.
> Have 3 stars... Maybe it'll amount to something.

Amazon **UK**

A MILLION
Random Digits

with 100,000 Normal Deviates

RAND